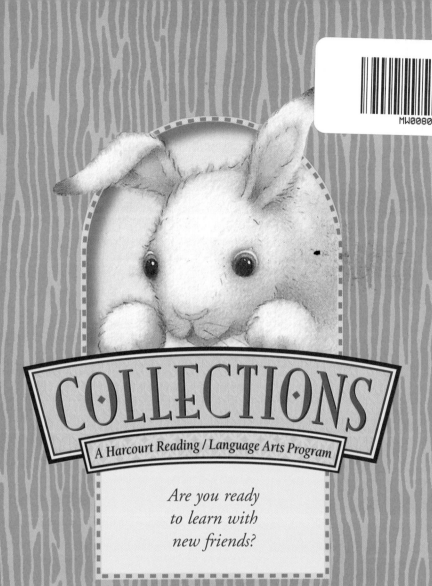

# COLLECTIONS

## A Harcourt Reading / Language Arts Program

*Are you ready
to learn with
new friends?*

# All My Friends

**Harcourt**

Orlando   Boston   Dallas   Chicago   San Diego

# COLLECTIONS

## A Harcourt Reading / Language Arts Program

## ALL MY FRIENDS

SENIOR AUTHORS

Roger C. Farr • Dorothy S. Strickland • Isabel L. Beck

AUTHORS

Richard F. Abrahamson • Alma Flor Ada • Bernice E. Cullinan • Margaret McKeown • Nancy Roser
Patricia Smith • Judy Wallis • Junko Yokota • Hallie Kay Yopp

SENIOR CONSULTANT

Asa G. Hilliard III

CONSULTANTS

Karen S. Kutiper • David A. Monti • Angelina Olivares

**Harcourt**

Orlando   Boston   Dallas   Chicago   San Diego

Visit *The Learning Site!*
www.harcourtschool.com

Requests for permission to make copies of any part of the work should be mailed to the following address: School Permissions, Harcourt, Inc., 6277 Sea Harbor Drive, Orlando, Florida 32887-6777.

HARCOURT and the Harcourt Logo are trademarks of Harcourt, Inc.

Acknowledgments appear in the back of this work.

Printed in the United States of America

ISBN 0-15-314474-2

5 6 7 8 9 10   048   2001

# All My Friends

**Dear Reader,**

Are you ready to meet some new friends? In **All My Friends**, there are characters waiting to meet you. They are ready to help you learn about the alphabet, being curious, reading signs, and words that rhyme. So go ahead, turn the pages, and say hello to your new friends.

Sincerely,

*The Authors*

The Authors

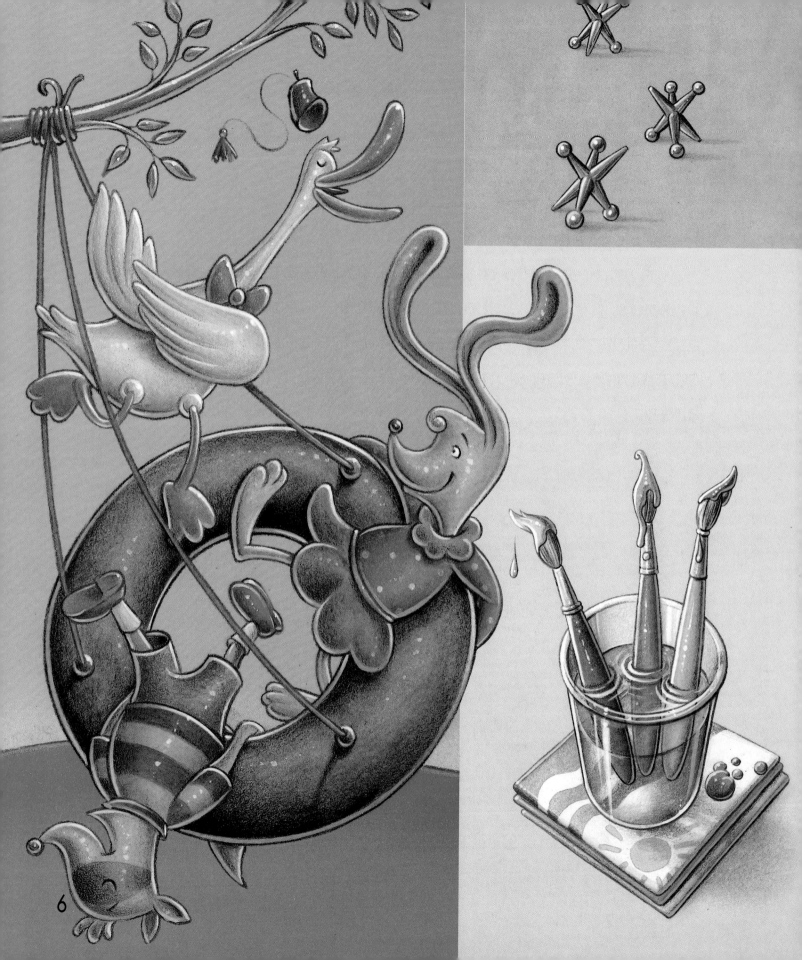

6

# Contents

# ALPHABET SOUP

illustrated by
Lori Lohstoeter

# Aa

# Bb

# Cc

# Dd

# Ee

# Ff

# Gg

# Hh

# Ii

# Jj

Jelly

# Kk

# Ll

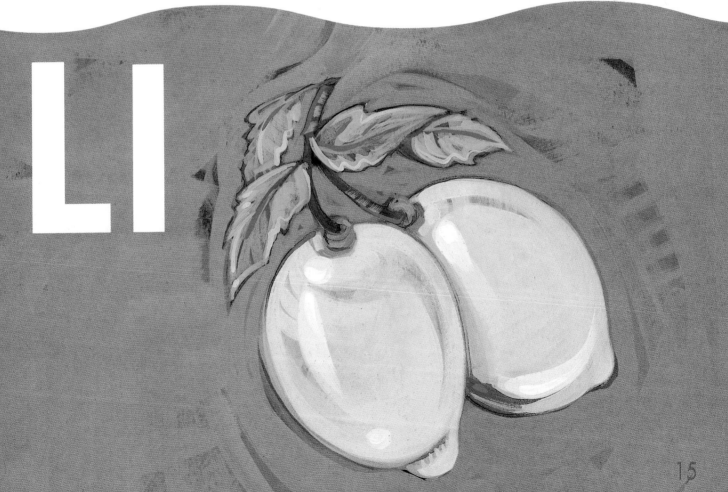

# Mm

# Nn

# Oo

# Pp

17

# Qq

# Rr

# Ss

# Tt

# Uu

# Vv

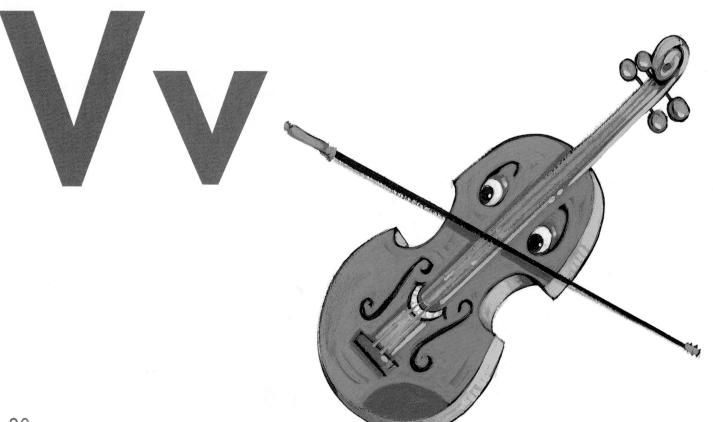

20

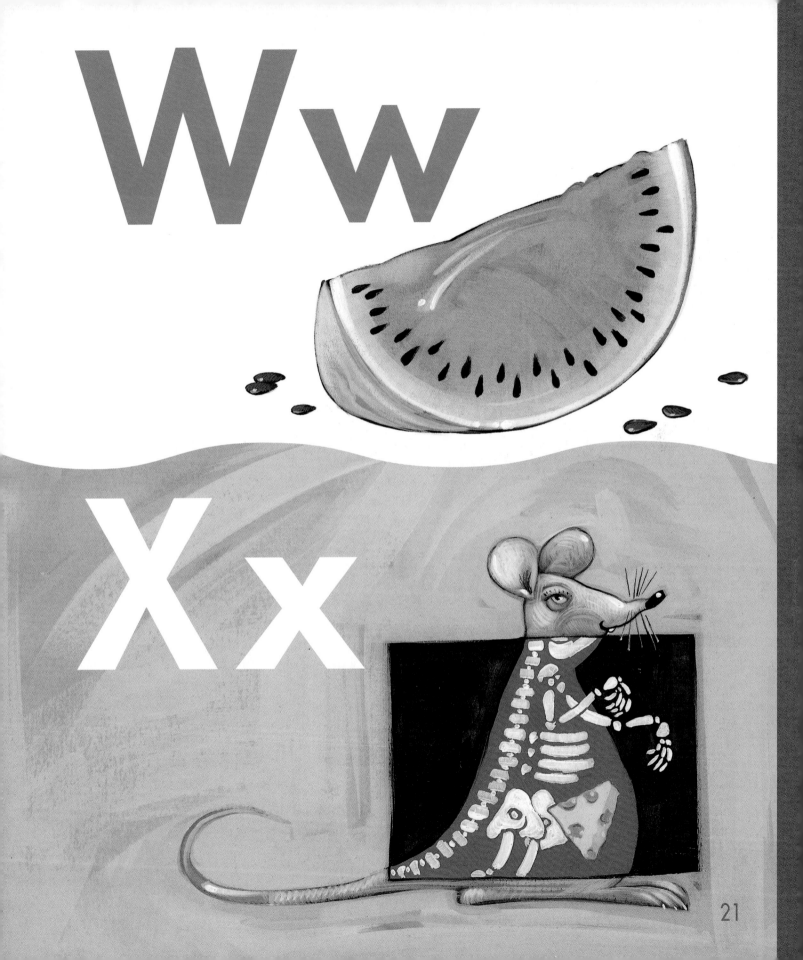

# W w

# X x

21

# Yy

# Zz

# Have You Seen

Have You Seen My Duckling?

Nancy Tafuri

Caldecott Honor
ALA Notable

# My Duckling?

Early one morning . . .

Have
you seen
my duckling?

34

Have you seen my duckling?

Have
you seen
my duckling?

Have you
seen my duckling?

# Have you seen my duckling?

43

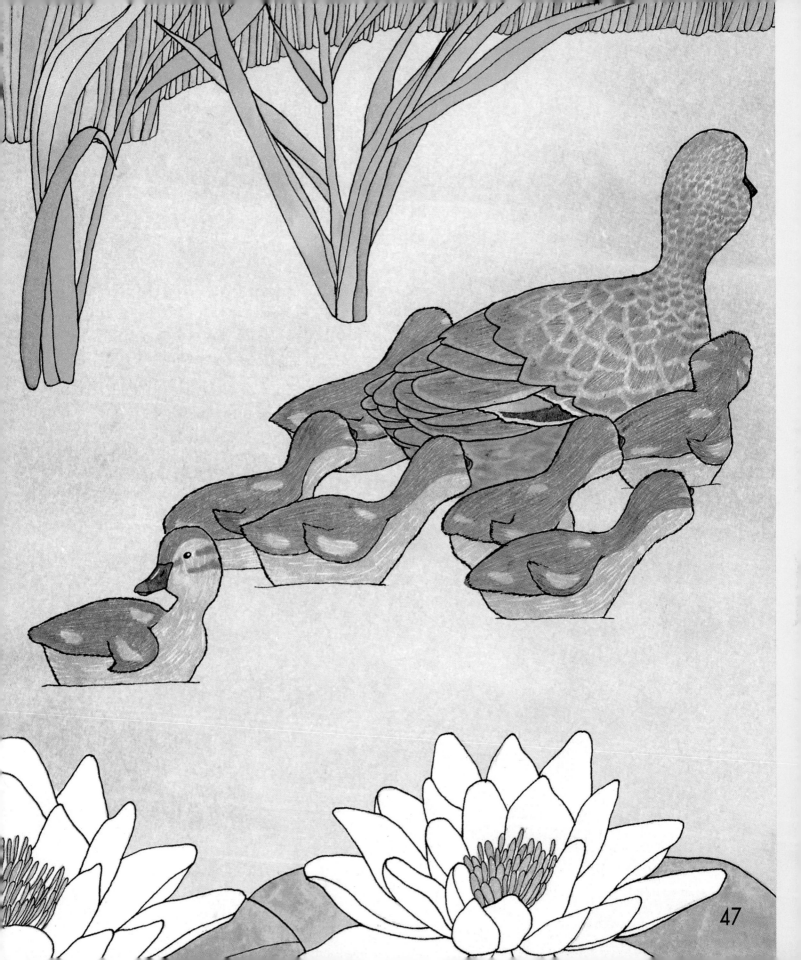

47

49

# Look what

New York Times
Best
Illustrator

# I can do

by Jose Aruego

Look what I can do!

I can do it too!

58

59

61

63

67

# Look what I can do!

74

Count with **Maisy**

Lucy Cousins

# Count with Maisy

# Lucy Cousins

Award-Winning Author and Illustrator

one
ladybug

**2**

two
flowers

# 3 three buckles

# 4

four
colors

# five
# pencils

**6**

six
fish

# 7

seven
steps

8

eight
ducks

9

nine
leaves

**10**

ten
fleas

How many flowers can Maisy count?

1  one

2 two

3 three

4 four

5 five

6  six

7 seven

8 eight

9 nine

10 ten

# I Read Signs

## by Tana Hoban

Award-Winning Author and Photographer

# Who Are You?

by Stella Blackstone
and Debbie Harter

WHO ARE YOU?

Stella Blackstone & Debbie Harter

# Who are you?

I'm a cat.

Who are you?

# I'm a bat.

# Who are you?

# I'm a whale.

# Who are you?

I'm a snail.

# Who are you?

I'm a hare.

# Who are you?

I'm a bear.

# Who are you?

# I'm a dog.

# Who are you?

# I'm a frog.

# Who are you?

I'm a goose.

# Who are you?

# I'm a moose.

# Who are you?

# You know who!

**Acknowledgments**

For permission to reprint copyrighted material, grateful acknowledgment is made to the following sources:

*Abbeville Press, Inc.*: *Who Are You?* by Stella Blackstone, illustrated by Debbie Harter. Text copyright © 1996 by Stella Blackstone; illustrations copyright © 1996 by Debbie Harter. Originally published in Great Britain by Barefoot Books Ltd., 1996.

*Atheneum Books for Young Readers, Simon & Schuster Children's Publishing Division*: *Look What I Can Do* by Jose Aruego. Copyright © 1971 by Jose Aruego.

*Candlewick Press, Cambridge, MA*: *Count with Maisy* by Lucy Cousins. Text copyright © 1997 by Lucy Cousins; illustrations copyright © 1992, 1994 by Lucy Cousins.

*Greenwillow Books, a division of William Morrow & Company, Inc.*: From *I Read Signs* by Tana Hoban. Copyright © 1983 by Tana Hoban. *Have You Seen My Duckling?* by Nancy Tafuri. Copyright © 1984 by Nancy Tafuri.

**Photo Credits**

Aaron Haupt/Photo Researchers, 102; Tana Hoban, 103-131

**Illustration Credits**

Marcus Pfister, Cover Art; Tracy Sabin, 6-7; Lori Lohstoeter, 8-23; Nancy Tafuri, 24-49; Jose Aruego, 50-75; Lucy Cousins, 76-101; Debbie Harter, 132-155

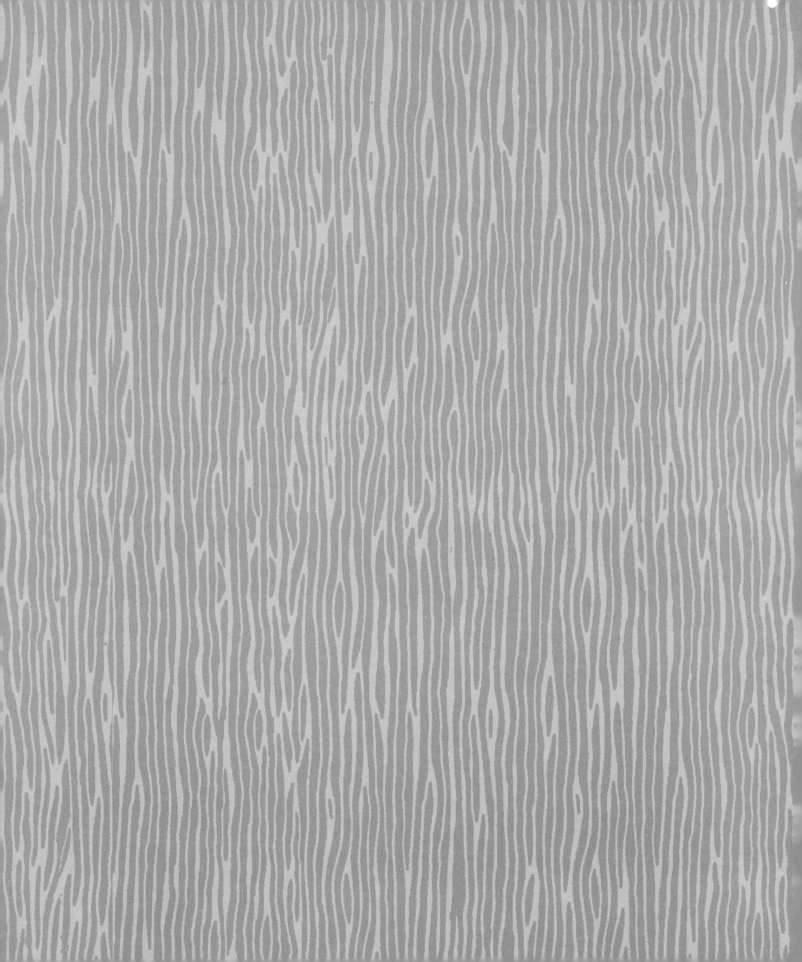